FASHION DOODLES

WRITTEN BY ANITA WOOD

ILLUSTRATED BY JENNIFER KALIS

GIBBS SMITH
TO ENRICH AND INSPIRE HUMANKIND

For Denise—fashionista and shopper extraordinaire!—AW

For my daughter Juliette, a true fashion lover and girly girl. You are especially sweet and helpful when I need it the most, and I am very proud of you.—JK

Manufactured in Dongguan, China in July 2014 by Crash Paper Company

First Edition
18 17 16 15 14   5 4 3 2

Text © 2014 Anita Wood
Illustrations © 2014 Jennifer Kalis

Published by
Gibbs Smith
P.O. Box 667
Layton, Utah 84041

1.800.835.4993 orders
www.gibbs-smith.com

Designed by Jennifer Kalis
Printed and bound in China

Gibbs Smith books are printed on either recycled, 100% post-consumer waste, FSC-certified papers or on paper produced from sustainable PEFC-certified forest/controlled wood source. Learn more at www.pefc.org.

ISBN 13: 978-1-4236-3607-6

This Book BELONGS to:

NAMe:
_____

Address:
_____

PHONE:
_____

e-mail:
_____

"Fashion fades, only Style Remains the Same."
- Coco Chanel

joy

L

Design
your own fashion labels and logos.

Lola Rose

Juliette's CLOSET

Design the sign for your fabulous fashion boutique.

You've made the cover of your FAVORITE FASHION MAGAZINE as this year's TOP NEW FASHION DESIGNER. FINISH the COVER.

It's FASHion Week in NEW YORK. What ARe Some of the designs you Will be PResenting on the Runway?

Finish Designing this invitation to your very first FASHION SHOW!

YOU'RE invited to

DESIGN the bottle and {label} for your line of perfumes.

Start Designing your SPRING Collection.

THE ROARING '20s

The use of mannequins became widespread during the '20s to show shoppers how to combine ready-made fashions and accessories.

Dress this mannequin using some of the fashions you see here.

'20s

RAYON STOCKINGS BECAME POPULAR AS A SUBSTITUTE FOR THE MORE EXPENSIVE SILK ONES, AND WERE OFTEN ROLLED DOWN DARINGLY CLOSE TO THE KNEE AND HELD IN PLACE BY A SILVER METAL GARTER. DOODLE SOME DESIGNS ON THESE GARTERS.

PREVIOUSLY MANY GARMENTS WERE FASTENED WITH BUTTONS AND LACING ONLY. DURING the '20s, METAL HOOKS AND EYES, ZIPPERS, AND SNAPS WERE INVENTED TO MAKE "BUTTONING UP" EASIER.

FINISH ADDING the TEETH to this ZIPPER.

COCO CHANEL

COCO CHANEL was the most influential woman in fashion in the twentieth century. She was one of the first women to wear trousers, cut her hair, and reject the constricting old-fashioned corset. Give this young Coco a fashion-forward "bobbed" hairstyle.

A FLAPPER'S HEADBAND WAS USUALLY ADORNED WITH TALL FEATHERS AND BEADED FRINGE. DECORATE THIS HEADBAND.

THE flapper
look included
A short drop-waist
DRESS with beading
and sequins, bobbed
hair, long beaded
necklaces, and a
close-fitting
cloche hat.

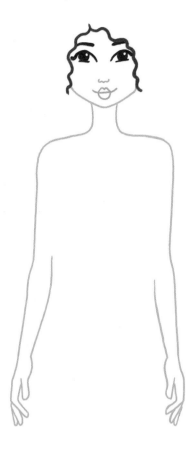

Give this mod wannabe the flapper treatment!

TOO SMALL TO CARRY ANYTHING BUT A COSMETIC COMPACT AND A COUPLE OF DOLLARS, BEADED PURSES WERE USED AS A FASHION ACCESSORY TO MATCH A FLAPPER'S DRESS. ADD SOME FANCY DECORATIONS TO THIS LITTLE NUMBER.

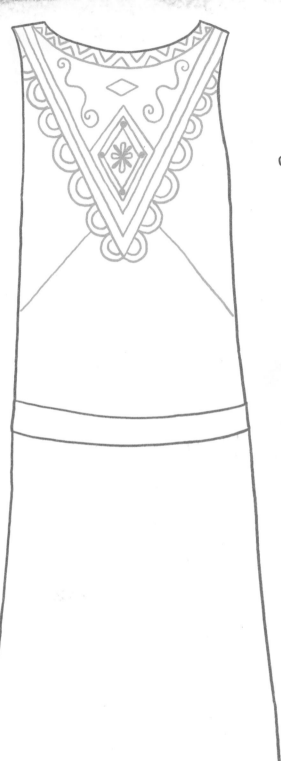

ART DECO was A POPULAR DESIGN style during the '20s, and EXTENDED to FASHION as well. WE'VE started the PATTERN FOR you—now FINISH iT.

Get CREATiVE with *Lipstick* makeup, hair extensions, and false eyelashes, to give this girl a complete makeover.

CoVeR THiS Hat with BuTTONS OF AlL SHapes and SizeS.

Fill in the fabric Swatch Squares below with Some complementary Patterns & Color Schemes, then design a DRESS that you'd like to use them on.

COVER THIS JACKET WITH PATCHES, BEADS, STUDS, OR BRAIDING.

Embellish these ballet flats with *JEWELS* and BEADS.

FASHiON has A Way of REpeating itself.

What styles do you pREdict to be popular 10 years fROm Now? DesigN an Example.

Doodle HENNA DESiGNS on these HANDS.

FUTURiSTIC, RoBOTIC, SCI-FI FASHIONS. DESIGN A FEW CRAZY OUTFITS AND ACCESSORIES.

ADD A FUN DESIGN ALONG the SEAMS of these STOCKINGS—maybe RAILROAD TRACKS, ANIMAL PAW PRINTS, or a tall, skinny ice-cream cone.

DECORATE these SANDALS
with your favorite flowers.

ONE of this matching pair of chandelier earrings is missing. DRAW it!

DECORATE this Platform PUMP with A Leopard PRINT DESIGN.

DECORATE these SNEAKERS with some SEQUINS & Glitter, OR MAKE them your FAVORITE COLOR.

ADD A TIGER PRINT TO THIS DRESS.

DECORATE this SKIRT
with designs of YOUR favoRite FRUITS.

DESIGN A PAIR of PANTS by Cutting A PATTERN out of A NEWSPAPER PAGE, THEN PASTE iT HERE.

Add some feathers to this mask to make it look like your favorite bird.

DESIGN some
FEATHER EARRINGS.

Fill in the fabric swatch squares below with some complementary patterns & color schemes, then design a skirt & top that you'd like to use them on.

The Nifty '50s

Ladies' hats were adorned with flowers, acorns, leaves, cherries, and polka dots.

Decorate this hat.

CORSages were Always ❀ WORN on the Lapel of A Lady's ❀ Suit or Coat that matched her HAT. ❀ Finish this one.

'50s

'50s

Fashionable Eyewear of the '50s known as "cat eye" glasses included wings in the outer corners of the frames. Meow! Fancy Earpieces were also part of the Look, and sometimes only one side of the eye frame was decorated for that extra-special Look. Add your Designer's touch to these frames.

FULL CIRCLE SKIRTS were often DECORATED with an APPLIQUÉ such as A Fancy Poodle (which led to the popular name "POODLE SKIRTS" for this '50s FASHION).

WHAT will YOU ADD TO THIS SKIRT?

Gloves were worn
all the time and you were never
properly dressed without them!
Add some fancy stitching to this pair.

'50s

DESIGN A PEARL CHOKER NECKLACE with MATCHING EARRINGS & A BROOCH.

Fur stoles and fur trim on collars and cuffs were totally '50s glamour statements. * Add some furry trimmings to this jacket.

'50s

'50s

Stiletto shoes with four- to five-inch pencil-thin, metal-tipped heels were a trademark of the '50s.

Design a pair.

'50s

Beehive hairdos—the higher, the better!
Give her a stylish do.

A PENCIL SKIRT, SWEATER SET, SCARF TIED AT THE NECK, Slicked-Back Ponytail, and SADDLE SHOES complete the look of a TYPICAL '50s Teenage girl. FINISH DRESSING HER WITH THESE PIECES OF CLOTHING.

'50s DOODLE A BUNCH of Polka Dots
on This HALTER DRESS.

'50s

Decorate these kitten heel pumps with a pouf of feathers.

'50s

A TYPICAL '50s TEENAGE BOY WOULD OFTEN DRESS in TiGHT jeans, LEATHER JACKET, and A white T-SHiRT. STYLE THIS GUY.

DESIGN A PAIR of EARRINGS USING SEASHELLS.

DRAW DIFFERENT PATTERNS ON these Friendship BRACELETS.

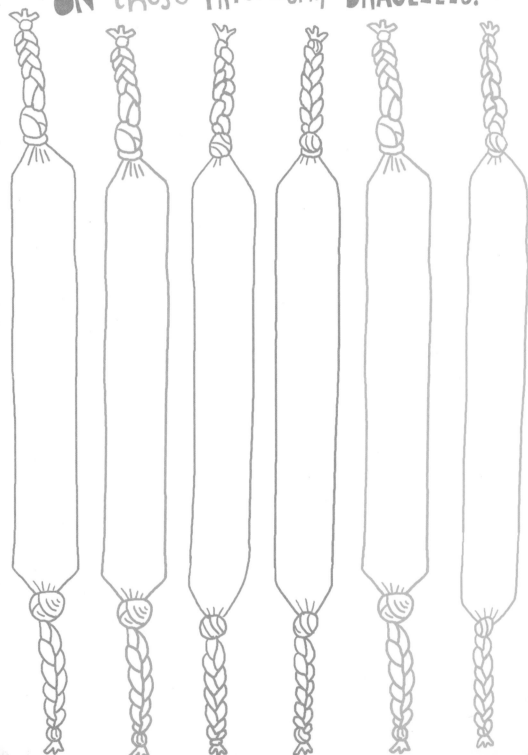

Design a name necklace with your name on it.

It's FASHion Week in PariS. What Are Some of the designs you Will be PResenting on the Runway?

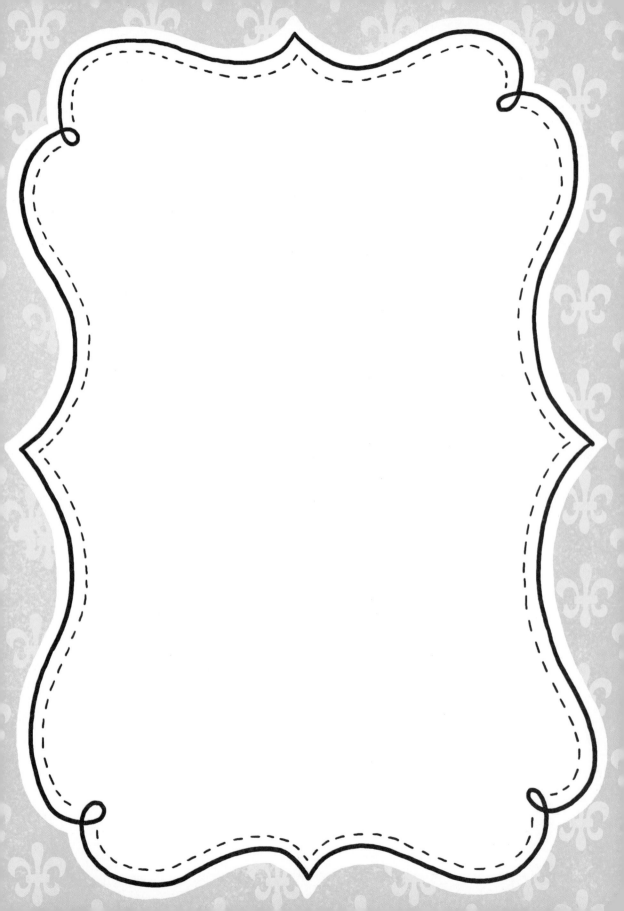

DESIGN your
VERSION of the
LBD
(Little Black
DRESS).

DECORATE the heels on these ANKLE BOOTS with SPIKES.

Fill in the fabric Swatch Squares below with Some complementary Patterns & Color Schemes, then design a SUIT that you'd like to use them on.

DESIGN A
jewel-encrusted buckle
for this belt.

"DRAW YOUR FAVORITE OUTFIT."

FiNiSh drawing the REST OF * * THiS PURSE.

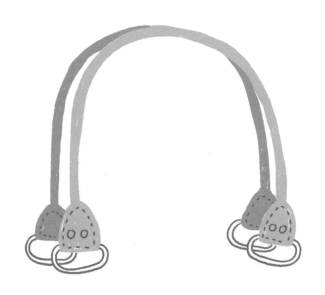

DECORATE these leggings with STRIPES or Some other PATTERN.

ADD a FUN DESIGN to thiS PAIR of TOE SOCKS.

DESIGN A SWEATER WITH A JEWEL, or CREW, NECKLINE.

DESIGN A KNIT TOP with A BATEAU (boat) NECKLINE.

Start Designing your Summer Collection.

DESIGN A V-NECK SWEATER.

DESIGN AN EVENING GOWN WITH A SQUARE NECKLINE.

DESIGN A CUTE Little DRESS with A FUN PRINT and A PETER PAN COLLAR.

DESIGN A DRESS FEATURING A KEYHOLE NECKLINE.

ADD A LONG, MULTISTRAND PEARL NECKLACE to COMPLEMENT the LOW BACK LINE of this DRESS.

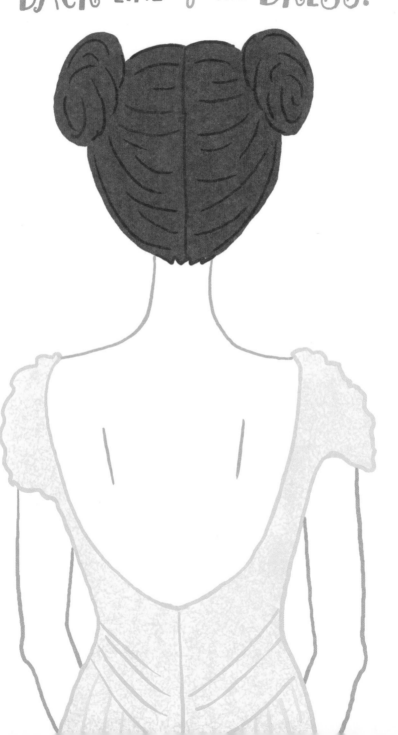

BLACK and WHITE with WILD GEOMETRIC DESIGNS is WHAT'S HAPPENING! DOODLE some SQUARES, DIAMONDS, CIRCLES, TRIANGLES, or ZIGZAGS all OVER THIS TOP and SKIRT.

Attach a swatch of DENIM in the SQUARE BELOW FROM an old, worn-out PAIR of jeans, and design a new pair on the next page. Will they be PLAIN OR PATTERNED?

Get this Wintertime fashionista Ready for her Ski trip. Design A toasty Warm outfit complete with furry hat, Scarf & Boots.

Give this GRECIAN GODDESS

A fancy pair of gladiator-style wedges with straps up to her knees.

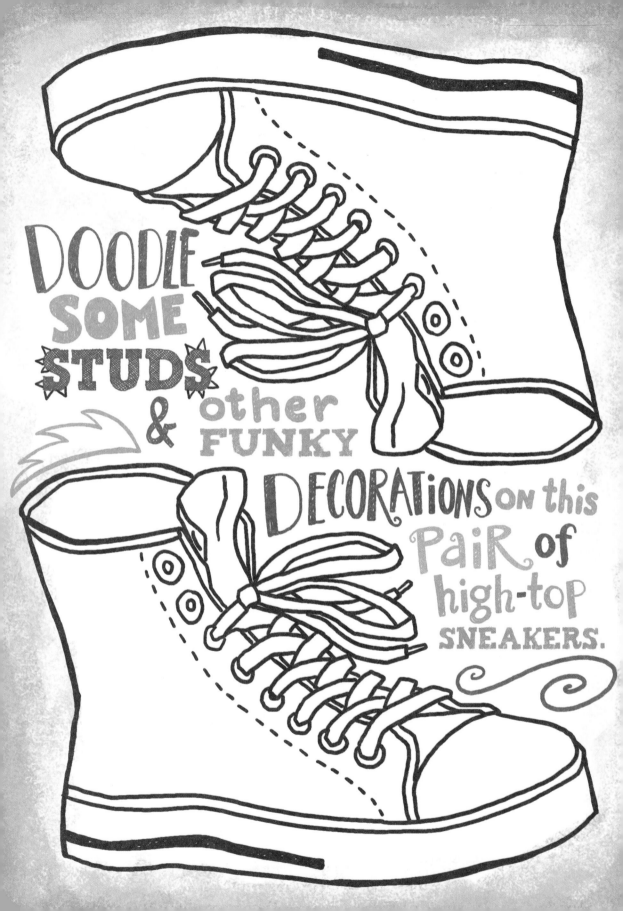

AHOY there!

Hook this cute little maritime sweetie up with a striped top and pants with a tiny anchor print all over them.

START DESIGNING YOUR EVENING GOWN COLLECTION.

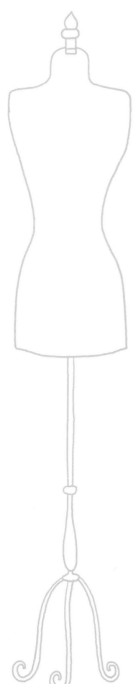

YOU JUST FOUND AN OLD TRUNK in YOUR GRANNY'S ATTIC. WHAT KIND of CLOTHING will you FIND INSIDE?

DESIGN A FABRIC PRINT with Butterflies & LAdybugs.

DOODLE SOME DESiGNS on these HOOP EARRiNGS.

THE MAD for MOD '60s

FASHiON DESiGNER MARY QUANT iNTRODUCED THE ▰ MiNiSKiRT & HOT PANTS ▱ (SHORT, SHORT SHORTS!) iN THE '60s. PUT YOUR OWN SPiN ON THESE FAB FASHiONS!

The Bikini came into FASHION in 1963 due to the POPULARITY of the musical BEACH PARTY. DESIGN YOUR OWN itsy-bitsy two-piece.

'60s

MISMATCHED PRINTS AND PATTERNS WERE EVERYWHERE! DESIGN AN OUTFIT USING DIFFERENT PATTERNS.

The Pillbox hat was made famous by First Lady Jacqueline Kennedy. Add a Lacy veil to this one.

BABY-DOLL DRESSES WITH SPAGHETTI STRAPS WERE TYPICAL '60s EVENING WEAR. DESIGN ONE OF THESE MINI CUTIES.

THE CHANEL SUIT WAS AN ICONIC '60s FASHION MUST-HAVE. THE SUIT FEATURED AN A-LINE SKIRT WITH A SHORT-WAISTED JACKET, AND INCLUDED DOUBLE POCKETS ON BOTH SIDES OF THE JACKET, WIDE TRIM, AND LARGE BUTTONS. ADD YOUR DESIGNER TOUCH TO THIS CLASSIC ORIGINAL.

Give this
HiP CHiCK
some
go-go boots,
HOT PANTS,
and
FISHNET
tights.

THE ANGEL DRESS WAS A  MICROMINI DRESS WITH A FLARED SKIRT and WIDE TRUMPET SLEEVES. DESIGN ONE.

Bell-Bottom Pants PANTS WERE OFTEN PAIRED WITH TIE-DYED SHIRTS & FRINGED BUCKSKIN VESTS. DESIGN AN OUTFIT FOR THIS HIPPIE DUDE.

GIVE THIS FLOWER CHILD A HEAD SCARF.

60s

'60s

FASHION ACCESSORIES of the '60s included PEACE SIGN JEWELRY, Love BEADS, Chain belts, and MEDALLION NECKLACES. CREATE A FEW PIECES.

60s

Ponchos and Moccasins were popular with the hippie generation. Hook this free Spirit up with some of your designs.

DESIGN AN OUTFIT with CAPRI PANTS AND A BUBBLE-SLEEVED BLOUSE; SHOES ARE OPTIONAL, BARE FEET PREFERRED.

'60s

INSPIRED by the "Fab Four" (The Beatles), BEATLE BOOTS WERE WORN BY YOUNG, MOD MEN OF THE '60s. They WeRe SHORT ANKLE BOOTS WITH LONG POINTED TOES. ...... DESIGN A PAIR.

SHORT RAINCOATS OR ANORAKS were also part of MOD FASHION. PAIR one up here with some matching galoshes.

'60s

DRAINPIPE JEANS (TODAY'S SKINNY JEANS) WERE A '60s fad made popular by actress Audrey Hepburn. ADD A fun PATTERN to these jeans.

VELVET mini dRESSES had matching Lace CollaRS that were either Round, OR long and Pointy with wide cuffs. Finish designing this dRess by adding the collars & cuffs.

'60s

FL✿WER P✿WER, BABY!

DOODLE A BUNCH OF DAISIES ✳ ON THIS MAXI COAT.

Dads always seem to get NECKTIES for Father's Day. Doodle a fun and CReative design on this one. →

COLLECT interesting
scraps of Lace and
Ribbon and paste
them here.

It's FASHION Week in LONDON. What ARe Some of the designs you Will be PResenting on the Runway?

Design Matching Outfits for you and your BFF.

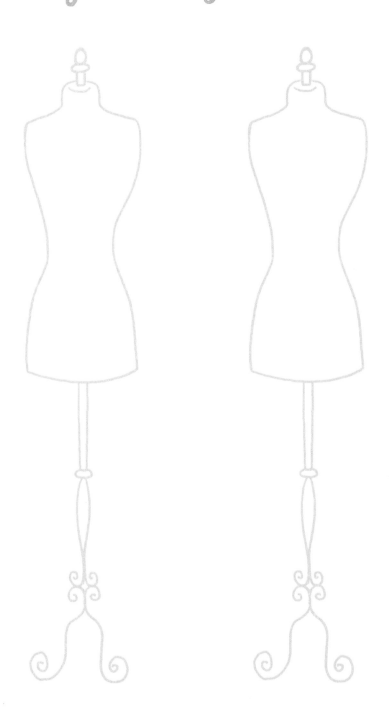

The "Shootie" is an interesting design mash-up of shoe and boot styles. Design an ankle-high shootie.

Start Designing your SHOE Collection.

Pick your favorite actress and design her gown to wear on the RED CARPET.

DOODLE A CHEVRON DESIGN ON THIS MAXI DRESS.

DESIGN THE DRESS OR SUIT THAT YOU WOULD WEAR ON THE RED CARPET.

DOODLE A SNAKESKiN
DESiGN ON THiS HANDBAG.

DESIGN A LONG, LAYERED NECKLACE with CHUNKY BEADS and TASSLES.

ADD Some Cute accessories to these flip-flops.

DESIGN A DRESS FOR THIS DEBUTANTE'S COMING-OUT PARTY.

GET HER OUT OF THOSE
* FUR SKiNS *
AND iNTO SOMETHING
FRESH &
* FUN.

CUT OUT ONE of YOUR FAVORITE FASHION STYLES FROM A MAGAZINE & PASTE it BELOW. HOW would you make it BETTER? CREATE YOUR own DESIGN ON the NEXT PAGE.

Start Designing your Fall Collection.

EVERY FASHION DESIGNER has their own brand of jeans. DESIGN your jean Label.

DESIGN A PAIR of PLATFORM SHOES with HOLLOW, SEE-THROUGH HEELS and SOLES to use as mini-aquariums. Don't FORGET TO ADD THE FISH!

Finish adding the face to this Cameo Necklace.

Design Some matching earrings
and a Ring to go with it.

THE GROOVIN' '70s

Boogie Shoes for Guys and Gals were BiG, CHUNKY PLATFORMS two to four inches High MADE of WOOD, CORK, or PLASTIC. FiNiSH ADDiNG the MASSiVE SOLES to THESE SHOES.

PAISLEY PRINTS were the HOT FASHION fad of the '70s. Doodle a paisley PRINT on this WRAP DRESS, which was also on trend during the disco decade!

LONG, STRAIGHT HAIR parted in the middle or with feathered bangs were how all the girls were wearing their hair. Give this girl some '70s hair.

BIG ROUND-frame and SQUARE-frame Glasses WERE HUGE!

The better to see you with, I suppose. Design a REALLY big pair of glasses — and give them a little bling while you're at it.

'70S

Miniskirts (thigh high), Midi Skirts (below the knee), or Maxi Skirts (to the ankle)— the choice was yours! DESIGN ONE of EACH.

'70S

Tiered skirts and drop-shoulder blouses, the peasant look, became popular in the mid-'70s. Doodle a FLOWER Design on the front of this BLOUSE.

'70s

The jumpsuit was A FASHION TREND WORN by both MEN & WOMEN. This one-piece Wonder Came in BRIGHT, FLASHY COLORS OR WILD PRINTS. HOW WILL YOU DecoRate This one?

The Bikini took a backseat to the new one-piece swimsuits that were starting to show up at the beach. Design a cute one-piece swimsuit.

'70S

Hip-hugger PANTS with Wide, FlaRed Bottoms were often paired with Skin-huggin' Leotards or Body Suits. Add a fun Design to this Styling Outfit.

'70S

CHOKER NECKLACES WERE OFTEN ADORNED with BIG FLOWERS. ADD A FLOWER TO THIS ONE.

'70s

CROP TOPS and HIGH-WAISTED PANTS were another fashion trend. Design an outfit for this hip '70s BABE.

'70S

SUNDRESSES WERE OFTEN WORN with Plain tees UNDERNEATH, CREATING A Layered Look.

FLORAL PRINTS Were a big thing in the '70s, So decorate this Sundress with A Bunch of fun flowers.

DESIGN A BIG, FLOPPY HAT TO GO ALONG WITH YOUR SUNDRESS.

'70S

PUNK FASHION CAME ON THE SCENE TOWARDS THE END OF THE DECADE, BRINGING WITH IT REALLY TALL SPIKED HAIR AND MULTICOLORED MOWHAWKS. HOOK THIS PUNK UP WITH A SPIKY DO!"

TORN JACKETS, RIPPED JEANS, and TEES WERE THE TYPICAL OUTFIT of the '70s PUNKER. DESIGN an OUTFIT— AND DON'T FORGET TO INCLUDE SAFETY PINS and a SPIKED DOG COLLAR TO WEAR AROUND THE NECK.

'70s

ANOTHER '70s FASHION TREND WAS STRIPES — EITHER BIG AND BOLD OR SMALLER AND THINNER. ADD SOME STRIPES TO THIS MIDI HALTER DRESS.

'70s

POLYESTER LEISURE SUITS IN BRIGHT COLORS & PLAIDS WERE POPULAR CASUAL DRESS FOR MEN. ADD SOME PLAID TO THIS SUIT & COMPLETE THE LOOK WITH SOME GOLD CHAINS.

'70S

ACTRESS DIANE KEATON popularized the "ANNIE HALL" Look in the Late '70s. This Look consisted of A wide-brimmed, droopy hat, Long vest, wide tie, baggy Pants, and a man's dress shirt. Re-create it for this ANNIE.

DOODLE A MIX OF DESIGNS, INCLUDING FL*WERS, STRIPES, AND DOTS, ON THIS SHIRT.

CUT OUT PICTURES of SOME of YOUR FAVORITE SHOES FROM A MAGAZINE & PASTE THEM HERE.

DESIGN A Few PaiRS of waterdrop EARRiNGS.

FASHiON has A way of Repeating itself.

What styles do you predict to be popular 50 years from now? Design an Example.

DESIGN A PAIR OF SPORTY SHOES—THAT LOOK LIKE FEET!

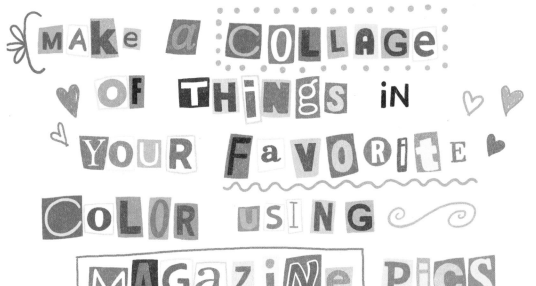

MAKe a COLLAGE OF THiNGS iN YOUR FaVORiTE COLOR USiNG MAGAZiNe PiCS.

DOODLE
A NATIVE
OR GEOMETRIC
DESIGN on this
TRIBAL COLLAR.

FINISH the Rest of this BUBBLE NeckLace.

Start Designing your Winter Collection.

DESIGN A CUTE PROM DRESS USING A SWEETHEART NECKLINE.

DESIGN A TOP WITH A SCOOP NECKLINE.

It's FASHION Week in MILAN. What ARE Some of the designs you Will be PResenting on the Runway?

THE, Like, TOTALLY '80s.

THE AEROBICS CRAZE IN THE EARLY '80S INSPIRED DANCEWEAR FASHION, WHICH CONSISTED OF LEOTARDS, LEG WARMERS, AND HEADBANDS, AND WAS ALSO WORN AS STREET GEAR. FINISH STYLING THIS "PHYSICAL" BABE.

"POWER DRESSING" for Women, ESPECIALLY in the WORKPLACE, included oversized SHOULDER PADS THAT WERE OFTEN attached inside a blouse, jacket, or dress by VELCRO STRIPS. THESE MONSTROSITIES MADE the Wearer Look like she was wearing a TRIANGLE BOX under her clothes. TURN THIS TRIANGLE into A SHOULDER-PADDED Piece OF CLOTHING.

THE VALLEY GIRL was, like, so stylish with her HEADBANDS, MiNi RA-RA SKiRTS (modeled after short, flared cheerleading skirts), and leggings.

Let's, Like, TOTALLY HOOK HER UP with, Like, A TOTALLY CUTE OUTFiT!

MISMATCHED EARRINGS WERE also AN '80s fad; the BIGGER and LONGER the EARRING, the BETTER. DESIGN an interesting PAIR.

'80s

OVERSIZED SWEATERS, T-SHIRTS, and SWEATSHIRTS with the NECKLINE Ripped out of them were totally HOT!

AND WORN OVER Leggings OR A MiniSkiRT MADE FOR AN even HOTTER LOOK!

ADD A Big, WIDE BELT to this Big TOP & FINISH With A MiniSkiRT.

HAWAiiAN SHiRTS, MADE POPULAR
by ACTOR TOM SELLECK in his TELEVISION SERIES
MAGNUM, P.I., BECAME A FASHION TREND FOR MEN.
SELLECK ALSO MADE MUSTACHES
POPULAR WITH THE GENTS! DOODLE SOME
TROPICAL FLOWERS ON THIS SHIRT AND GIVE
THIS MAGNUM WANNABE-A-HAIRY LIP.

COWBOY BOOTS WERE POPULAR IN THE EARLY '80s, EVEN AMONG NONCOWBOYS. GIVE THIS URBAN COWBOY A FANCY PAIR OF KICKERS AND A

HAT.

PaRTLY as a THROWBACK to the '50s COLLEGiate Look, the PREPPY FASHiON style included a FAMiLY CReST on the Pocket of a Single- or double-bReasted BLaZeR, Complete with engraved GOLd BuTTONS. Add a CReST and Some buttons to this jacket and doodle a design on the buttons.

'80s

COMPLETING THE PREPPY LOOK
WERE CANDY-STRIPED SHIRTS, LOAFERS,
AND ARGYLE SWEATERS & VESTS.
FINISH the ARGYLE PATTERN ON THIS VEST.

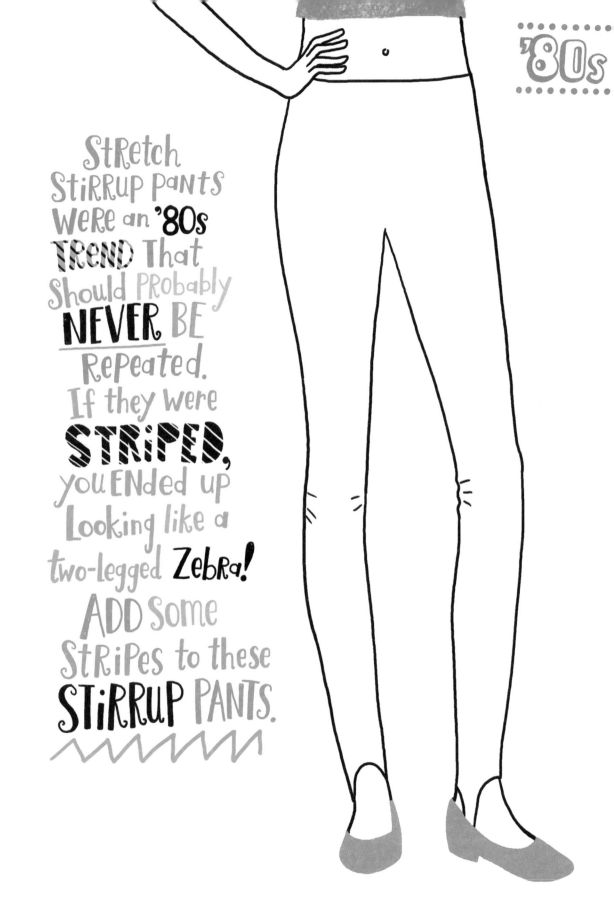

StRetch StiRRUP PaNtS WeRe an '80s TReND That Should PRobably NEVER BE Repeated. If they were STRiPED, you ENded uP Looking like a two-legged ZebRa! ADD Some StRiPes to these STiRRUP PANTs.

GIRLS JUST WANTED TO HAVE FUN!

And part of the Street urchin look made POPULAR by POP STAR MADONNA were FingerLESS FiSHNET GLOVES, tulle SkiRtS, HEADBANDS, BANANA CLiPS, and LARGE CRUCiFiX JeweLRy. DRAW SOME of these "MATERiAL GiRL" ACCESSORiES.

'80s

Lots and Lots of thin bangle bracelets were an '80s must. Dress this arm up with tons of bangles.

THE '80s WAS THE DECADE OF HAIR BANDS & ROCK STARS. STYLE THIS ROCKER UP WITH A MASSIVE DO!

'80s

'80s

HOW MANY cans of HAIRSPRAY Do You think THiS Look REQUIRED? DRAW the CANS.

THE CLASSIC FARMER BIB OVERALLS WERE FASHIONED INTO "SHORTALLS," SPORTING SHORT PANTS INSTEAD of LONG. FINISH THIS PAIR.

'80s MICHAEL JACKSON inspired TEENAGERS to wear STUDDED LEATHER JACKETS and SUNGLASSES at night. DOODLE SOME STUDS ON THIS JACKET.

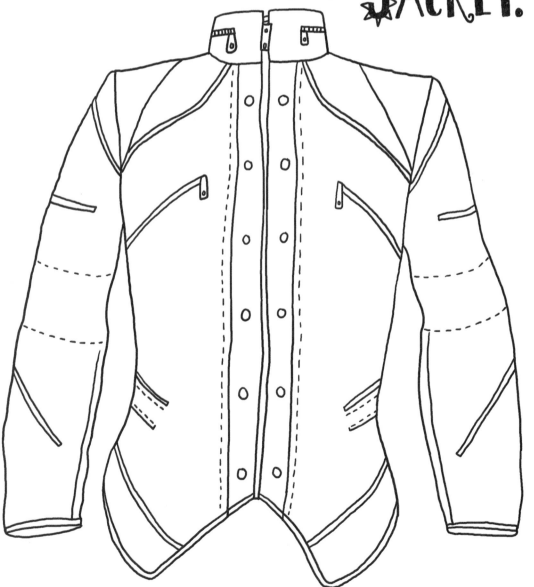

'80s

It's "HAMMER TIME"!
PARACHUTE PANTS, OFTEN WORN BY BREAK-DANCERS, WERE REALLY BAGGY PANTS WITH BRIGHTLY COLORED PATTERNS ON THEM.
ADD YOUR OWN COLOR AND PATTERN TO THIS PAIR.

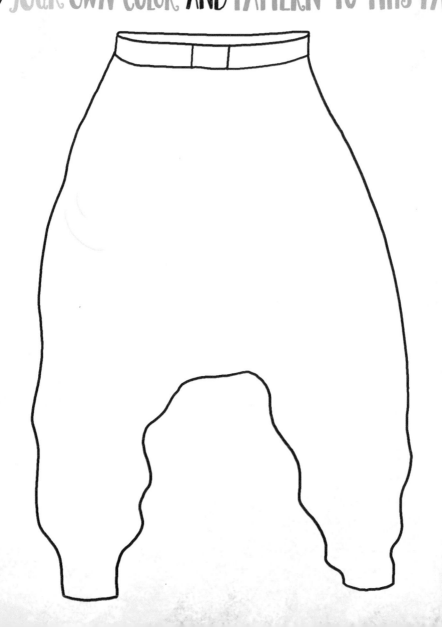

'80s

BABY-DOLL DRESSES were OFTEN PAIRED with BLACK TIGHTS, White SLOUCH SOCKS, and WHITE SNEAKERS. COMPLETE this look by ADDING her DRESS.

DECORATE THIS BIB NECKLACE WITH LOTS OF PEARLS AND JEWELS.

FINISH DESIGNING THIS RING AND BRACELET CHAIN.

Design a fabric print with HEARTS.

Start designing your
BRIDAL collection.

Give this Latin princess a Quinceañera gown to wear for her fifteenth birthday party Celebration!

Give this
tiny dancer
a fashionable
tutu.

DESIGN a BUNCH of Buttons in different SHAPES & SIZES.

DOODLE SOME fingernail ART ON THESE NAIL FORMS.

DESiGN A BUNCH
of fun
HAIRPiECES and
ACCESSORiES.

DECORATE
THiS HAT
FOR THE
KENTUCKY
DERBY.

ADD SOME DECORATION TO THIS FASCINATOR (A MINIATURE ALTERNATIVE TO A HAT.)

ONE PiECE

Start Designing your Beachwear Collection.

BaNDeau

Boy SHORTS

Bikini

STRaPLESS

Halter

DESIGN A COOOL RING THAT YOU CAN WEAR ON YOUR THREE MIDDLE FINGERS.

Country Western Chic!
This snap-buttoned Western shirt needs some decoration. Doodle some flowers on the yoke and pockets.

Give this Leather vest some Long Fringe & Fancy Silver Buttons.

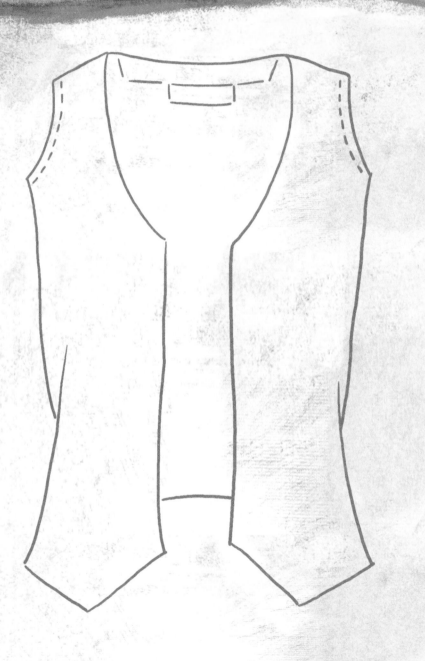

DECORATE this HATBAND...

with SOME TYPICAL WESTERN DESIGNS.

Add a mini saddle to the top of this purse.

Finish this Charm Bracelet, using some of the Charms you see here—or Creating some of your Own.

Give this Western belt buckle some cowgirl bling!

Give this little COWgirl a cute Sundress and pair of BOOTS.

NOTES...